Casey's Greatness Wings:
Teaching mindfulness, connection & courage to children

Written by
Tammi Van Hollander LCSW, RPT

Illustrations by
Annie Wilkinson

© 2018 by Tammi Van Hollander, LCSW, RPT, Main Line Therapy, LLC
All Rights Reserved. Visit us @ www.mainlineplaytherapy.com.

Dedication
This book is dedicated to my loving, amazing, inspirational grandmother, Lois Elkman whose unconditional love is seen and felt.

"How do you spell 'love'?" - Piglet
"You don't spell it...you feel it." - Pooh
— A.A. Milne

Table of Contents

1) Letter to Storytellers..4

2) How To Use This Book...8

3) "BACK" Story® Tips & Techniques...10

4) Title Page..11

5) Part One: The Comforting Hug...13

6) Part Two: Casey's Greatness Wings..31

7) Hand Movements Glossary..44

8) Activities...49
   - Greatness List..50
   - Greatness Wings..51
   - The Worry Elephant..52
   - Grandmother Butterfly..53
   - Explaining Mindfulness to Children...54

9) For Mental Health Professionals, Teachers and Counselors...................56

10) Acknowledgements...58

11) About the Illustrator..60

Letter to Storytellers

Dear Storyteller,

Casey's Greatness Wings is an interactive, multi-sensory experience of mindfulness, love, connection & resilience. The story is based on Dr. Janet Courtney's FirstPlay Kinesthetic Storytelling® method, which kids call "BACK Stories™".

Imagine a story that you can actually HEAR and FEEL. This book offers an important inspirational message of celebrating one's greatness. They are called "BACK Stories™" because the story is experienced on the child's back. I use Dr. Courtney's story "The Magic Rainbow Hug" regularly in my sessions with parents and children to promote bonding, playfulness, creativity, and sensory input.

Other benefits of nurturing touch include an increase in focus, calmness and social skills. When you do this activity with your child, you are increasing attachment, bonding, connection, and empathy while also teaching appropriate boundaries. *Casey's Greatness Wings* was written to empower children and strengthen the parent/child bond.

In the story, Casey compares himself to the other caterpillars and worries that he will never be as good as anyone else. He is unable to let go of his worries and enjoy life. Children see their differences as a setback or a challenge instead of finding a way to embrace what makes them unique. Casey always had greatness and beauty inside of him, but he needed the Wise Grandmother Butterfly to help him see and "feel" his true greatness. Casey the caterpillar did not feel like he was "good enough." There are SO many children who are hard on themselves, feel misunderstood, and believe that life is unfair.

There is nothing more valuable than parents and caregivers honoring the relationship and staying attuned and connected to the child, especially when things feel hard and chaotic. This is the most important time to stay mindful in the relationship and not join the chaos. I encourage every storyteller reading this book to practice the "Calm and Relax" breathing that the Wise Grandmother Butterfly teaches Casey. Each breath in, think "I am calm," and on the exhale think "I am relaxed." The more you can practice mindfulness techniques, the better you will be at providing patience, love, and compassion to your child. There is a guide to teaching children mindfulness in the back of the book. Also included in the book are activities to ignite greatness and tackle worries.

Children have so many gifts of greatness, but they are often unable to find them. They can feel "stuck" or spiral into negative thinking. Anyone working with children has a vital role in recognizing and teaching children about their positive qualities.

This is a symbolic tale about honoring greatness and celebrating YOU!

It is a Trans-for-ME-tion story.

A little about my Wings of Greatness...

When my mother passed away, she let my sisters and I know that we will always be connected by rainbows and butterflies. The Wise Grandmother Butterfly represents my mother as well as my 93-year-old grandmother who provide me with unconditional love, compassion and resilience. I am so grateful to all the people in my life who never let me forget that I am special and that I could do anything I put my mind to. Having someone believe in you is the most important gift we can give our children. This capacity and insight to believe in ourselves can take us on endless courageous adventures.

"What is greatness?" you may ask. Greatness can be whatever you want it to be. To me, it is a place inside of you where core beliefs of positive qualities radiate through everyone around you. I think about all the people who have touched my heart and filled my voids throughout my life. They gave me the inner wealth to shine when I would feel like my light was fading. Greatness is the color of rainbows that fill your heart and soul. I was introduced to the concept of greatness when I attended an intensive certification course to be a trainer in The Nurtured Heart Approach®. Learning this approach was transformative and amplified the greatness I saw in my clients, family and most importantly in myself.

There is additional information in the back of the book about The Nurtured Heart Approach® where you will find resources on how to ignite your child's greatness. I want to honor all the storytellers for taking the time to celebrate your child and build a trusting relationship of love and connection that will be passed down from generation to generation.

To your greatness,
Tammi

How to Use This Book

This is an interactive book to read and do the BACK Story™ on your child's back. Although the main character Casey is written as a male in this book, the name is GENDER NEUTRAL, so you can ask the child what gender Casey is and adapt the story to them. The story has two parts that can be read separately or together. Part One: *The Comforting Hug* focuses on mindfulness, connection and courage and Part Two: *Wings of Greatness* celebrates and honors Casey's many strengths and the strengths of the child. The greatness is installed into their mind, heart, and body (or back).

The BACK Story™ is an added, playful bonus. It is a full sensory experience increasing attachment, kindness, and empathy. Always ask your child for permission to do the story. "Is it okay for me to draw a story on your back?" If they say no, you can read it to them or they can do it on a stuffed animal. Each "greatness word" has a heart to indicate for you to draw a heart on your child's back. There is a glossary of hand movements on page 44 and you will get helpful hints on each page so you can do the interactive storytelling without interfering with the message of the story. The recommended hand movements are emphasized in the story as the words that are CAPITALIZED.

Have your child sit up in front of you, so you have access to their back and the book can be next to you. You can cross your legs or have your child sit between your legs. Make sure they do not sit on your lap or too close because you need to be able to do the activities on their full back. This is not a massage and no lotion is needed. This is done with the child fully clothed. You may not want them to be wearing too many layers so they are able to FEEL the story. Also, make sure that you are not wearing any rings or bracelets that can scratch your child.

Most importantly, have FUN and be PLAYFUL with your child. Try to find a time when you can be alone with your child so you can give them your undivided attention. Set aside a special time to "unplug" from any distractions and "plug in" to time with your child.

You can teach a sibling to do this on their sibling. It is a great way to teach about appropriate touch, bonding and empathy. This can also be done in a circle with family members, group work or in a classroom if given permission for the children to touch the other.

Make sure the storyteller first checks in with themselves to make sure they are fully present before beginning the story experience with the child. I often use the quote by Howard Glasser that "Children read energy like braille." Never underestimate a child. They are fully aware if you are being authentic and connected or if your mind is elsewhere.

❖ *Mental health professionals, teachers, healthcare providers, massage therapists, occupational therapists, speech therapists and other storytellers will find helpful suggestions on how to use this book with your students or clients on page 56.*

"BACK" Story®
Tips & Techniques

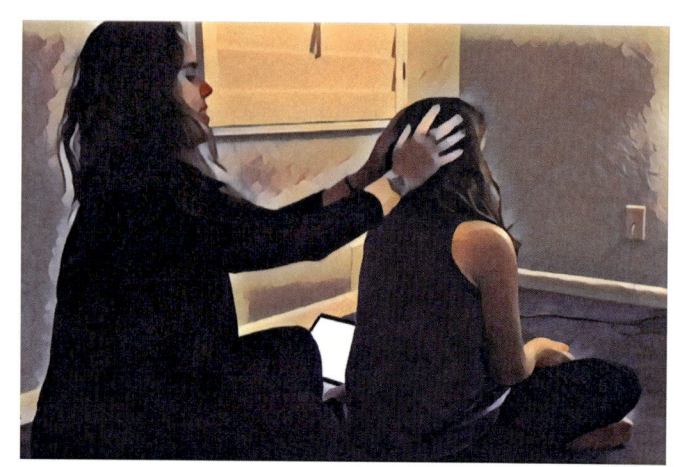

There is a glossary of hand movements on page 44. They are only suggestions as the main goal is to have fun and do whatever movements that feel intuitive or let your child direct you. For more information: you can watch a demonstration video of the storytelling experience on my YouTube channel under Tammi Van Hollander. I suggest that you watch this video without your child since it is important for you to not be plugged into a computer when you are doing this activity. The child's only focus should be on the words (hear), the Back Story™ (touch) and the illustrations in the book (see). Some children may prefer to close their eyes and use their imagination to picture the story in their mind.

The Story of Casey's Greatness Wings:
Teaching mindfulness, connection & courage to children

Written by
Tammi Van Hollander, LCSW, RPT

Illustrated by
Annie Wilkinson

PART ONE
THE COMFORTING HUG

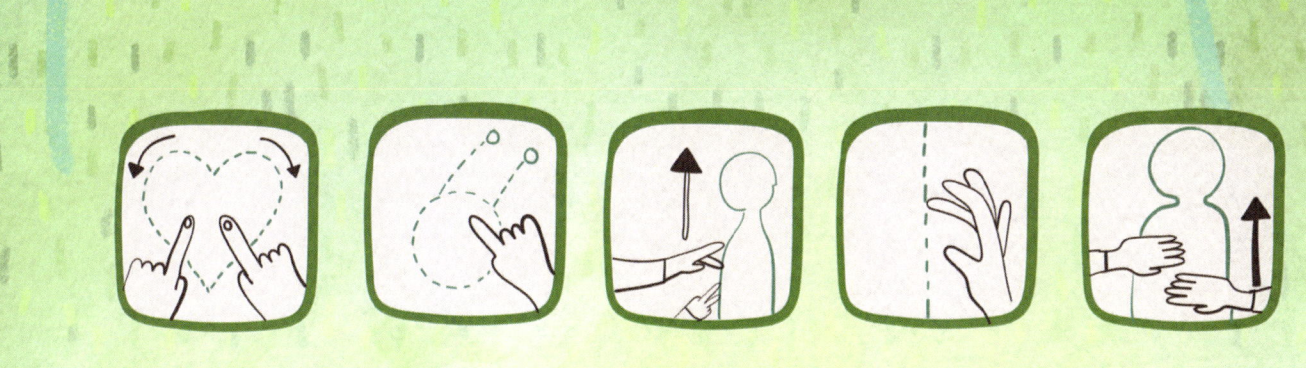

One day a KIND♥ little CATERPILLAR named Casey CRAWLED through his busy meadow home. The meadow sounded like a musical band with birds singing, bees buzzing, and crickets chirping.

The other caterpillars DANCED and played in the sunny meadow with the TALL GREEN GRASS.

Casey's friends asked him to dance, but Casey didn't know how to dance. He felt different and was afraid of looking silly. Casey watched from a distance.

He knew he was a very SMART♥ caterpillar, but Casey believed that his family and friends were smarter, better, and more liked than him.

Casey felt jealous of his brother because he was the BOOKWORM in the family. He knew the answer to everything.

Casey's sister was the STRONGEST♥ CLIMBER in the meadow.

And even Casey's friend, Sam was a good DANCER and had all the right moves.

Suddenly, all of his thoughts made Casey feel both sad and confused.

These negative thoughts made Casey's mind feel VERY, VERY, VERY HEAVY.

Do you know how heavy Casey's thoughts felt? As heavy as an elephant!

In fact, Casey felt like he was stuck underneath a huge, giant grey ELEPHANT.
Casey didn't know how to get the elephant off his back.

He tried to SHAKE him off

He tried to PUSH him off.

He tried to BRUSH him off.

Struggling with the elephant made Casey feel very tired ... tired ... tired... He then fell into a deeeeeep sleep.

When Casey awoke, his antennas perked UP and his sleepy eyes widened. A Wise Grandmother Butterfly had magically appeared.

Casey stared at her SPARKLING wings. They were a beautiful mix of yellows and oranges that SPREAD across her back.

Grandmother Butterfly smiled at Casey and said, "I have watched you fighting to get that heavy elephant off your back."

"You could have given up, but you didn't ♥."

"You could have taken your sadness and frustration out on others, but you didn't ♥."

"You have tried to find a way to defeat that heavy elephant and that shows me that you are very BRAVE ♥."

Although Grandmother Butterfly recognized his EFFORT ♥, Casey still felt that heavy elephant on his back.

He let out a SIGH.

At that moment, Grandmother Butterfly gave him a MAGICAL SMILE and COCOONED HER WINGS AROUND him tightly. There was no room for elephants when Grandmother Butterfly was around. Casey felt like he was in a warm silky blanket.

As Casey felt her LOVING♥ WINGS AROUND HIM, he began to SPIN and SPIN like a tornado. He did not know what was happening, but he TRUSTED♥ Grandmother Butterfly as he SNUGGLED in even closer.

He shut his eyes and took a DEEP BREATH IN through his nose and OUT from his mouth.

With each breath in he thought, "I AM CALM" and with each breath out, he thought, "I AM RELAXED" IN and OUT ... IN and OUT... CALM and RELAXED.

He went deep inside his mind and with each breath the elephant got smaller and lighter. So light, that Casey now imagined the elephant drifting off into the clouds.

His thoughts started to settle DOWN and he felt CALMER♥ than he had felt in a very long time.

Casey felt a magical warmth from the tips of his antennas to his HEAD, to his FACE, and throughout his BODY.

Imagine that warmth in your body? Maybe you feel it in your chest, your face or your toes.

He noticed in that moment of STILLNESS♥, that he could PAY ATTENTION♥ to how his body felt more relaxed. And because of that, Casey was AWARE♥ that his thoughts were more relaxed too.

In the CALM♥, Casey realized that his mind had been playing tricks on him. He recognized he was the boss of his thoughts and feelings. Casey closed his eyes and took another DEEP BREATH IN and said with CONFIDENCE♥

"I am good enough just as I am."

Casey had the COURAGE♥, to boss the elephant and say, "Get off my back! Get off my mind!" He felt POWERFUL♥ knowing he could control his thoughts. He pictured all the things that made him HAPPY♥

What makes you happy?

In that joyful moment, Casey felt different. He had changed.

Grandmother Butterfly's comforting hug was really a COCOON!

PART TWO
CASEY'S WINGS OF GREATNESS

Knowing that Casey changed his way of thinking, the Wise Grandmother Butterfly RELEASED her graceful wings and the warm sun rays KISSED his smiling face.

Casey then looked down into the SPARKLING pond and saw his reflection. He couldn't believe his eyes.

He had wings! Casey had REAL WINGS!

Wow, Casey the Caterpillar had become a BEAUTIFUL♥ butterfly!

Suddenly, the Wise Grandmother Butterfly pulled out a magical feather.

The tip of the feather STROKED his delicate wings, as she painted a word onto them.

The first word Grandmother Butterfly wrote was B-E-A-U-T-I-F-U-L. Beautiful. In that moment, he truly felt BEAUTIFUL ♥.

The second word was K-I-N-D. Kind ♥. Casey's eyes lit up.

The Grandmother Butterfly continued to PAINT different greatness words on Casey's wings. He let out a joyful giggle.

What other greatness words should we add?

Casey flew over the flowering meadow with a HAPPY♥ and PEACEFUL♥, HEART♥. He could not wait to see his friends and show them that everyone has greatness wings – we just need the courage to set them free.

In her magical hug, she taught him to see the beauty♥ in the world and, most importantly the BEAUTY ♥ in himself. Grandmother Butterfly knew that everyone, including Casey, would have days when the elephant would come to visit.

Grandmother Butterfly said, "When you are having a hard day, breathe in and out, and read the words of GREATNESS ♥ aloud. You are ONE OF A KIND♥ and celebrate all the things that make you SPECIAL♥."

Casey shouted,

"Remember that you are GREAT♥.

Remember that you are SPECIAL♥.

Remember that you are BRAVE♥.

You are not alone!" he said PROUDLY♥."

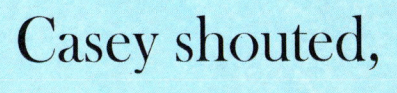

Casey teaches us it's important to recognize that all feelings are okay and to remember that you can't have a RAINBOW without RAIN.

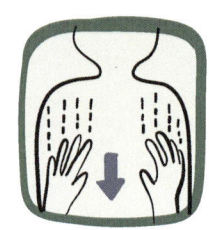 # Hand Movement Glossary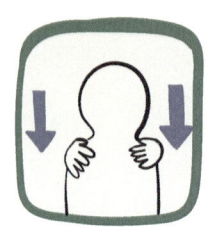

The hand movements are really intuitive. These are only suggestions. The best advice is to read through this glossary a few times. Practice the movements on a pillow or a partner. When it is time to read the story to the child, just do what feels right for you and the child. Feel free to make up the hand movements as you go along. There will be reminders on each page. There is no wrong way to do the BACK™ Story. You may want to just repeatedly stroke the child's back diagonally with gentle pressure in a fluid motion. This is a calming rhythmic movement for you and your child. This is great when there are flying motions and during the mindfulness part of the story. Remember all the greatness words have a heart, indicating that you draw a heart on the child's back and the CAPITALIZED words are recommendations for BACK™ Story movements. Be creative and let your child be creative with ideas and what feels best on their back.

 **HEART**: Using finger pads of both hands, start in the middle of the back. Move both hands upward than outwards and down making a wide heart shape and ending the motion of both hands coming together.

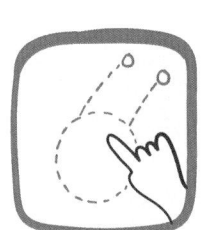 **CATERPILLAR**: Draw a caterpillar on child's back. Ask the child what gender Casey is. As you draw, tell the child what you are drawing. "Here is the body." Ask child "What else does the caterpillar need?" Then move on to whatever the child directs you to do (i.e.: antennas, eyes, mouth, legs).

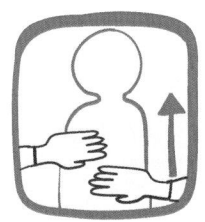 **TALL GREEN GRASS**: With flat palms, start at bottom of back and move upward up the back.

 **ELEPHANT**: With both hands apply pressure to the child's back, you can also rest your body on top of your child's back for them to feel that deep pressure.

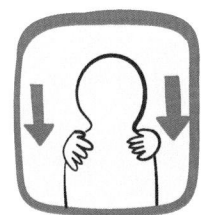 **DEEP SLEEP**: Give child a hug and gently rub their arms downward.

 **MAGICAL WARMTH**: This is based on body scan as you touch the child's head, face, shoulders and move your hands down the body. You can say each part of the body as you touch the child. "Feel the warmth in your shoulders, feel it in your arms...down to your toes."

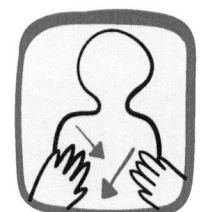 **FLYING**: Move hands diagonally in a sweeping motion one hand at a time (this can also be done during the mindfulness section when Casey is embraced in Grandmother Butterfly's arms).

 **Butterfly's Warm EMBRACE**: Wrap your arms around your child from behind. Feel free to kiss their head too!

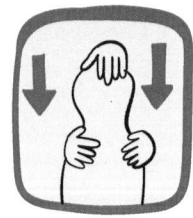 **QUIET MIND**: Gently place both hands on the child's head.

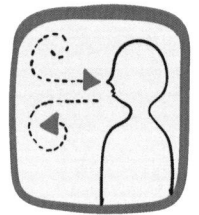 **CALM/QUIET BREATHING**: Breathe in through the nose and out through the mouth.

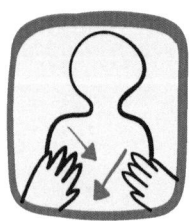 **The Grandmother Butterfly's RELEASE**: Hug child from the back and then release the hug. Then with both hands make a diagonal sweeping motion from top to bottom on back.

  **GREATNESS WORDS**: With two fingers draw in cursive, scribble or make a heart, saying greatness words aloud. This is a great opportunity to ask child "What other words should we add?" Add words the child suggests and storyteller can also add words. "You show the greatness of kindness when you shared you toy with your brother."

ENDING OF STORY: Make a RAINBOW on child's back and then with finger pads make RAIN.

End with a BIG HUG.

Activities Included

- **Greatness List:** This list is used for the two activities. Encourage the child to think of their own greatness words and you can add ones to the list.

- **Greatness Wings Activity Worksheet** can be completed with you and the child. The child can make their own butterfly or you have my permission to make copies of the template on page 51. Make a Greatness Wall in your home, classroom or office. Make sure there is a behavior that is linked to their greatness word, so the child can understand how they possess this character trait. The Wise Grandmother Butterfly gave many recognitions to Casey on page 9 of the story. Reread the story on your own and listen to the Grandmother Butterfly's recognitions. Reminder: recognitions and greatness words have a heart next to them indicating to draw a heart on the child's back to "install" their greatness.

- **The Worry Elephant:** The second activity includes a worksheet where the child can write their worries inside the elephant. When children write down their worries, they remove them from their head to the paper. The child can then find ways to "boss back" the elephant and feel empowered that they have control of their thoughts and feelings. Boss back worries like Casey, "Get off my back," "Get out of my mind." The worries can be rated on a scale of one to ten and help your child and student recognize that their negative thoughts are not true and that their mind is good at playing tricks on them.

- **Draw a picture of you and someone who reminds you of Wise Grandmother Butterfly.** Once the child draws a picture, have the child use the greatness list to include traits they love about that person. For deeper therapeutic value, you can also ask them to mark the qualities on the list that they wish that person had more of. For example, the child may use a parent or teacher and put all the things they love about the parent, but then may say "I wish my parent was more CALM and PATIENT."

- **Explaining Mindfulness to Children:** This page helps you explain mindfulness to children and deepen their understanding of Casey's experience in the book. This page encourages children to use mindfulness techniques to quiet their minds and bodies and decrease their worries.

What words are on your Greatness Wings?

Circle and then add words to butterfly wings.

Kind	Encouraging	Mindful
Brave	Relaxed	A Problem-Solver
Loving	Calm	Generous
Creative	Happy	Focused
Playful	Funny	Motivated
Fun	Responsibile	Hard Worker
Talented	Inspiring	Magical
Athletic	Kind-Hearted	_____
Strong	Clever	_____
Helpful	Comforting	_____
Thankful	Wise	_____
Thoughtful	Honest	_____
Forgiving	Hopeful	_____
A Good Friend	Self Control	_____

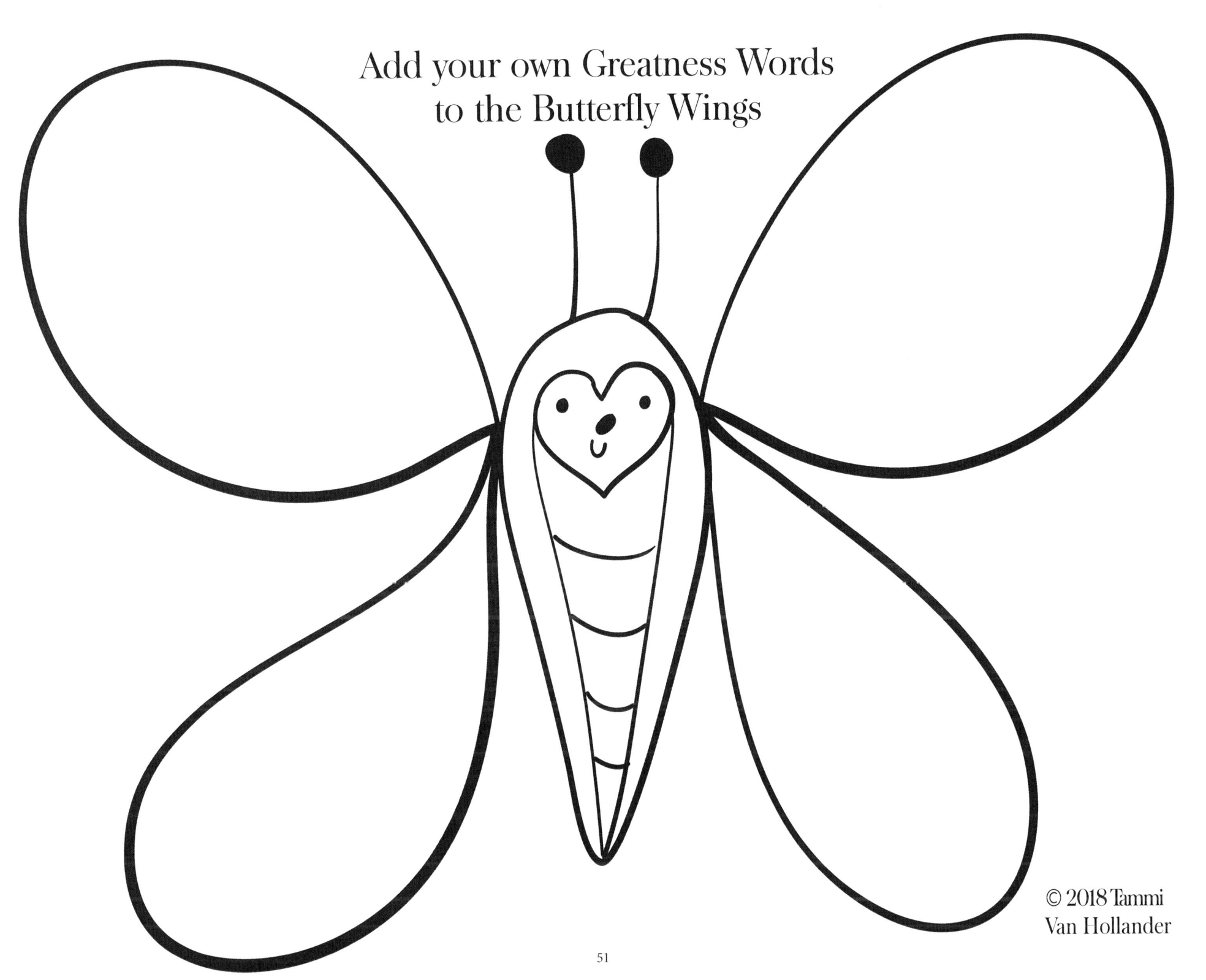

Draw a picture of you and someone who reminds you of Wise Grandmother Butterfly.
Write what you love most about them.

© 2018 Tammi Van Hollander

Explaining Mindfulness to Children

Mindfulness is simply NOTICING what is happening right now. It is being AWARE of how your body communicates through your five senses. This is what you see, smell, hear, taste and feel. Mindfulness is also noticing what your mind is doing. The Buddhists call the busy mind the "monkey mind". When we practice mindfulness, we open the mind to creativity and provide a safe space of KINDNESS, COMPASSION and ACCEPTANCE. When we live in the PRESENT moment, we do not have the regrets of the past or the worry of the future weighing us down (like a heavy elephant).

Repetition! The more you practice mindfulness, the better you get at it. If you often worry, you are probably a master worrier, because you have been doing it for years.

When we practice mindfulness regularly, we can retrain our brains to become calmer, more focused, and compassionate.

Deep Breathing

When our minds are busy, angry, stressed or worried, it is difficult to think clearly, access our thinking brain (prefrontal cortex) and calm down. Deep breathing brings oxygen to the brain, so you can think clearly and quiet the mind. Grandmother Butterfly teaches Casey to inhale "I am relaxed " and exhale, "I am calm." Breathe in through your nose and out through your mouth. You can also imagine smelling flowers (inhale) and blowing out birthday candles (exhale). Practice visualizing your worries drifting off in the clouds (like the elephant). Bubbles are also a great way to practice mindful breathing. You will notice Casey blowing a bubble in the story when he thinks about the things that make him happy. Have the child inhale and slowly blow the biggest bubble they can. Feathers are also great for breathing and a reminder of the feather Grandmother Butterfly paints on Casey. Take a feather in the cup of your hands and blow it into the child's cupped hand. This game could be done together or with the whole family or classroom.

Body Scan

It is important to understand that we hold tension, feelings and energy in our bodies. The body scan brings focus and awareness to what our bodies are trying to tell us. In the story, as Casey is breathing, the storyteller guides Casey to feel the magical warmth throughout his or her body, from head, to face to shoulders.

For Mental Health Professionals, Teachers, Guidance Counselors, Occupational Therapists, and other professionals working to support children

If you are a professional with a mandate not to touch children, you can just read the story to the child or you have other creative options. The child can do the story on a stuffed animal or they can even draw it. I recommend that therapists, teachers and other professionals teach this to the parent/caregiver. For example: The therapist will sit on the floor next to the parent and child and the therapist will model it on a stuffed animal and read the story while coaching the parent on how to do the interactive parts of the story. In my office, the child normally has his/her hands in the sandtray while the parent does the story on the child's back. The sand is an added tactile experience that helps to quiet the body and mind.

As a professional, you always want to make sure you have permission to touch your student or client. When introducing this book to your clients, families or the classroom, it is important to understand why this work is important. When we give caring and nurturing touch, we release the love and connection hormone called oxytocin which then decreases our stress hormone, cortisol. FirstPlay Kinesthetic Storytelling® increases the oxytocin for you and the child at the same time. When we teach children to do these stories on each other, we are teaching healthy boundaries and the benefits of safe touch. I recommend Dr. Janet Courtney's book *Touch in Child Counseling and Play Therapy: An Ethical and Clinical Guide*. This book is helpful to deepen your understanding of the power of touch and how it could be used safely and ethically in clinical settings.

The Nurtured Heart Approach® has been a true inspiration of this book. Check out Howard Glasser's book *Transforming the Intense Child* for more ideas on how to give recognitions to your child and for you to get a deeper understanding of this powerful, transformative approach. NHA® is being used in schools, therapy practices and homes all over the world. The recognitions are important in order to ensure success. When we give children our full attention and verbalize what we see (or verbalize what they are doing), we are planting the seeds for children to flourish.

"We all have greatness in our 'hardware' – we all signed up for greatness when we came into this life and we are simply learning to awaken it in one another." ~ Howard Glasser

You can learn more about The Nurtured Heart Approach® by visiting www.childrenssuccessfoundation.com.

Acknowledgments

There are SO many people that I want to thank for helping me on this journey to bring Casey's Greatness Wings to life. First, I want to thank Dr. Janet Courtney for her dedication, guidance, patience, and mentorship throughout this process. She inspired me to create this project and introduced me to the beauty and therapeutic power of the FirstPlay Kinesthetic Storytelling®.

To my magical, inspirational daughter, Gabby, my encouraging, loving son Aden, and my wise and compassionate fiancé, Neal King, who are the loves of my life. When it comes to "greatness" you three can write the book.

To my AMAZING grandmother and best friend, Lois Elkman. Thank you for being my Wise Grandmother Butterfly.

To my mother, Carol Schwartz who is in heaven communicating to me through rainbows and butterflies.

To Stanley Elkman, my grandfather, who was a role model with a generous heart.

Thank you to my father, Elliot Schwartz, who always believed that I could do anything I put my mind to.

To my sisters and my awesome nieces and nephews. Simone & Sage Levy were influential in moving this book forward.

I am SO thankful to my amazing friends and colleagues who have influenced where I am today.

To my childhood best friend, Sylvie Viola. You have always been there to hold my hand through it all. I do not know what I would do without you. You are a life saver and I'm so blessed to have you in my life.

David Crenshaw, you have been a true mentor and friend and you make my heart smile. You have taught me the true value of play therapy.

Eliana Gil has been a long-time inspiration in my play therapy career and I am grateful for her support and recognition.

I have to give special shout outs to my encouraging play therapy angels: Deanne Gruenberg, Jenn Taylor, Robert Jason Grant, & Dorothy Derapelian who took time out of their busy lives to give me feedback and guidance.

Thank you, Howard Glasser, for creating The Nurtured Heart Approach®. This approach has been transformative to so many children and families.

Lastly, thank you to my clients who have been my best teachers. They have helped me with the story of Casey and the "BACK Stories™" with their creative, thoughtful, curious minds.

I am beyond GRATEFUL and truly BLESSED for the awesomeness of
the people in my life who have touched my heart and given me the wings to fly.

 About The Illustrator: Annie Wilkinson is the youngest of eight children and the mother of two. She works in a variety of mediums including traditional and digital, creating bright and whimsical illustrations for both books and products. She also has a background in design and as a fine artist, two skills that she calls upon quite frequently when illustrating. She is currently working on her own picture book.

CPSIA information can be obtained
at www.ICGtesting.com
Printed in the USA
BVRC020452210319
543309BV00015BA/21